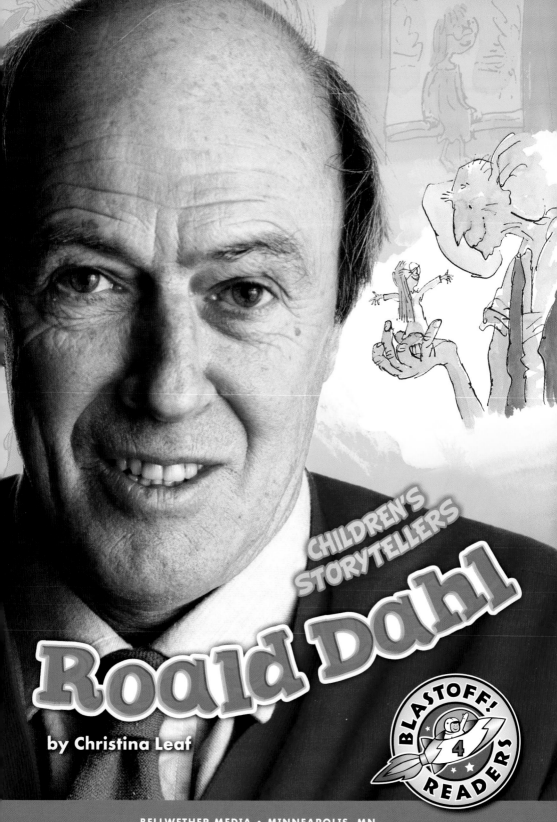

CHILDREN'S STORYTELLERS

Roald Dahl

by Christina Leaf

BLASTOFF!
4
READERS

BELLWETHER MEDIA • MINNEAPOLIS, MN

Note to Librarians, Teachers, and Parents:

Blastoff! Readers are carefully developed by literacy experts and combine standards-based content with developmentally appropriate text.

Level 1 provides the most support through repetition of high-frequency words, light text, predictable sentence patterns, and strong visual support.

Level 2 offers early readers a bit more challenge through varied simple sentences, increased text load, and less repetition of high-frequency words.

Level 3 advances early-fluent readers toward fluency through increased text and concept load, less reliance on visuals, longer sentences, and more literary language.

Level 4 builds reading stamina by providing more text per page, increased use of punctuation, greater variation in sentence patterns, and increasingly challenging vocabulary.

Level 5 encourages children to move from "learning to read" to "reading to learn" by providing even more text, varied writing styles, and less familiar topics.

Whichever book is right for your reader, Blastoff! Readers are the perfect books to build confidence and encourage a love of reading that will last a lifetime!

This edition first published in 2016 by Bellwether Media, Inc.

No part of this publication may be reproduced in whole or in part without written permission of the publisher. For information regarding permission, write to Bellwether Media, Inc., Attention: Permissions Department, 5357 Penn Avenue South, Minneapolis, MN 55419.

Library of Congress Cataloging-in-Publication Data

Leaf, Christina.
  Roald Dahl / by Christina Leaf.
    pages cm. – (Blastoff! Readers: Children's Storytellers)
    Summary: "Simple text and full-color photographs introduce readers to Roald Dahl. Developed by literacy experts for students in kindergarten through third grade"– Provided by publisher.
  Includes bibliographical references and index.
  Audience: Ages 5-8
  Audience: K to grade 3
  ISBN 978-1-62617-270-8 (hardcover: alk. paper)
  1. Dahl, Roald–Juvenile literature. 2. Authors, English–20th century–Biography–Juvenile literature. 3. Children's stories-Authorship–Juvenile literature. I. Title.
  PR6054.A35Z735 2016
  823'.914–dc23
  [B]
                            2015000855

Printed in the United States of America, North Mankato, MN.

Table of Contents

Roald Dahl is one of the world's best-loved storytellers. He used his wild imagination to write funny and sometimes scary **novels** for kids.

Roald loved children. He understood how kids think and knew what they like to read. Because of this, his books are still popular today.

A Hard Childhood

Roald Dahl was born in Llandaff, Wales, on September 13, 1916. He had a big family. He grew up with many siblings.

Llandaff, Wales

When Roald was just 4 years old, his father and a sister passed away. His mother was left to care for six children. These **tragedies** may have **influenced** Roald's sadder stories.

When Roald was 9 years old, he attended **boarding school** in England. Life at school was hard. Roald had mean teachers and lived far from his family. But he had fun playing games and pulling pranks.

Young Roald also wrote letters to his mother every week. This began his love of writing.

"A little nonsense now and then is relished by the wisest men."
–Charlie and the Chocolate Factory

Roald's first jobs after school let him travel the world. Tanzania, Greece, Iraq, and Egypt were some of the countries he visited. He collected stories during his adventures.

fun fact

One of Roald's early jobs was flying as a fighter pilot in World War II. He also worked as a spy.

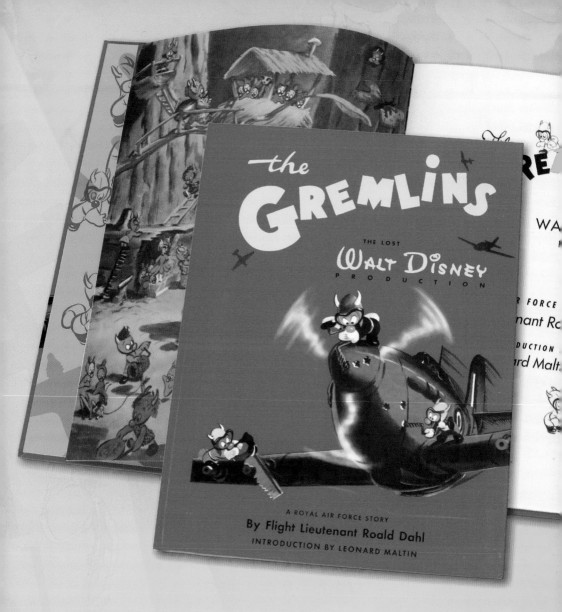

One story was about creatures called
gremlins. They caused planes to break
down. Roald's gremlin idea was sent
to **movie producer** Walt Disney. He
wanted to turn it into a film.

The Gremlins story that Roald wrote was never made into a movie. However, it was **published** as a children's book with some success. Roald continued to write. He published short stories and a novel for adults.

Roald did other types of writing, too. He wrote and hosted a television mystery **series**. He also wrote a play.

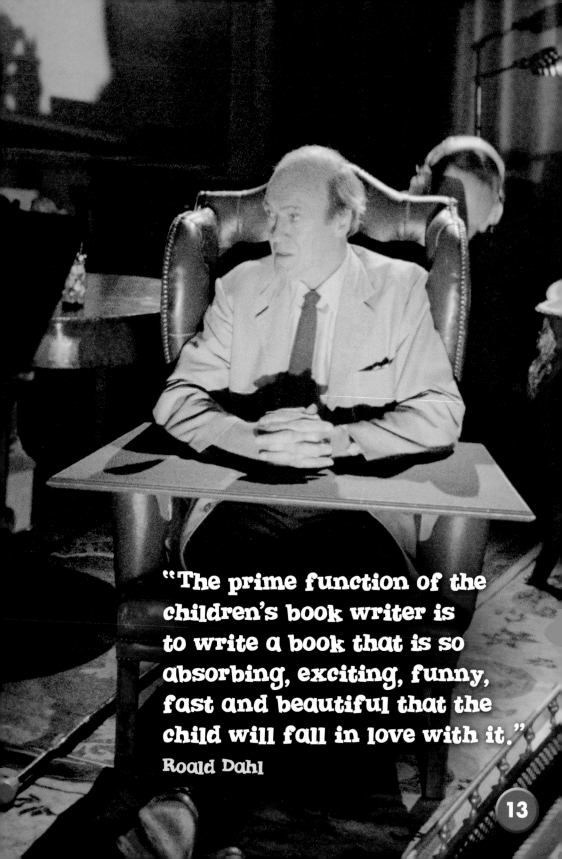

"The prime function of the children's book writer is to write a book that is so absorbing, exciting, funny, fast and beautiful that the child will fall in love with it."

Roald Dahl

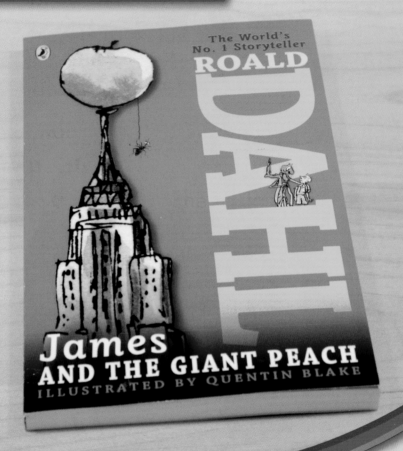

In 1961, Roald published a book for children called *James and the Giant Peach*. It got good **reviews** but did not sell well at first.

Roald was **discouraged**. But he still worked on another novel for children. This one was about a boy's trip to a chocolate factory. In 1964, *Charlie and the Chocolate Factory* was published to great success.

fun fact

Roald first wanted Maurice Sendak to draw the pictures for *Charlie and the Chocolate Factory*. Maurice became famous for his book *Where the Wild Things Are*.

Scrumdiddlyumptious Stories

Roald's books for children are popular because they are imaginative. Their pages are filled with magical wonders like dream-making giants and marvelous chocolate factories.

SELECTED WORKS

James and the Giant Peach (1961)

Charlie and the Chocolate Factory (1964)

Fantastic Mr. Fox (1970)

Charlie and the Great Glass Elevator (1972)

Danny, the Champion of the World (1975)

The Twits (1980)

The BFG (1982)

The Witches (1983)

Boy: Tales of Childhood (1984)

Matilda (1988)

Some of the magic in Roald's books is in his words. He twisted words to make new meanings. He also created silly but **expressive** new words, such as *filthsome* and *scrumdiddlyumptious*.

Roald's books can be scary. Adults are sometimes **cruel** and children are put in danger. But Roald felt that kids' books should always be funny. He made frightening problems so unbelievable that they became silly.

Happy endings also balance the scary parts. Mean and **greedy** characters always get what they deserve. Good children escape trouble by using their wits.

POP CULTURE CONNECTION

The musical *Matilda* first opened in 2010. This version of Roald's popular book included songs and dances. People love this live version of Roald's classic story!

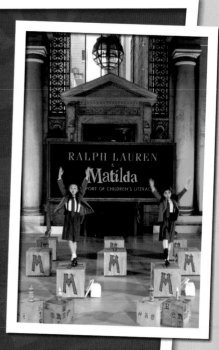

"If you are good life is good."
–Matilda

A Giant Influence

More than two **decades** after Roald's death, his work is still loved. Fans celebrate Roald Dahl Day on the author's birthday each year.

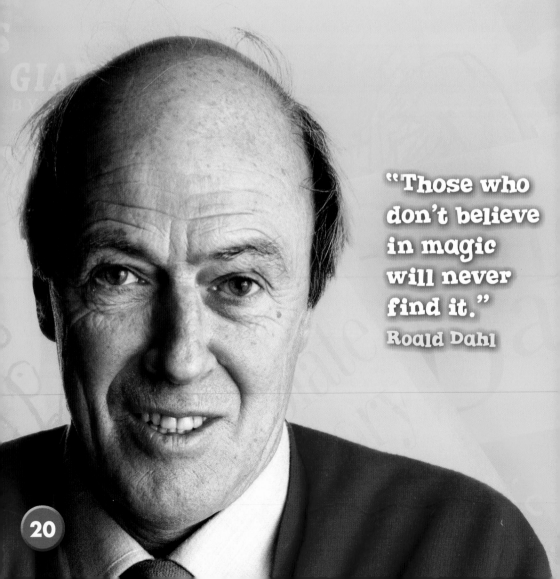

"Those who don't believe in magic will never find it."

Roald Dahl

IMPORTANT DATES

1916: Roald Dahl is born on September 13.

1943: *The Gremlins* is published.

1961: *James and the Giant Peach* is published.

1964: *Charlie and the Chocolate Factory* is published.

1971: The movie *Willy Wonka and the Chocolate Factory* opens.

1977: Roald begins working with illustrator Quentin Blake. Quentin later creates drawings for most of Roald's books.

1982: Roald publishes his first book of poetry for children, called *Revolting Rhymes*.

1984: *Boy: Tales of Childhood*, a collection of stories based on Roald's childhood, is published.

1989: Children vote *Matilda* as the winner of the Red House Children's Book Award.

1990: Roald passes away on November 23.

There is also an award called The Roald Dahl Funny Prize. It was named to honor his influence on humor in kids' books. Roald shaped children's writing in such a big way that he will not soon be forgotten.

Glossary

boarding school—a school at which the students live during the school year

cruel—ready to hurt others without feeling bad

decades—periods of ten years

discouraged—made less hopeful or confident

expressive—describing what it means

greedy—selfish and wanting more than what is fair

gremlins—imaginary little creatures that cause planes to break down, especially planes in the United Kingdom's Royal Air Force

influenced—caused something to happen or change

movie producer—someone who oversees the making of a movie

novels—longer written stories, usually about made-up characters and events

published—printed for a public audience

reviews—articles that discuss the quality of something

series—a number of things that are connected in a certain order

tragedies—disastrous events

To Learn More

AT THE LIBRARY

Dahl, Roald. *Boy: Tales of Childhood*. New York, N.Y.: Farrar, Straus, Giroux, 1984.

Guillain, Charlotte. *Roald Dahl*. Chicago, Ill.: Heinemann Library, 2012.

Rosen, Michael. *Fantastic Mr. Dahl*. New York, N.Y.: Penguin Group, 2012.

ON THE WEB

Learning more about Roald Dahl is as easy as 1, 2, 3.

1. Go to www.factsurfer.com.

2. Enter "Roald Dahl" into the search box.

3. Click the "Surf" button and you will see a list of related web sites.

With factsurfer.com, finding more information is just a click away.

Index

The images in this book are reproduced through the courtesy of: Tony Evans/ Timelapse Library Ltd/ Getty Images, front cover, p. 20; CB2/ ZOB/ Wenn.com/ Newscom, front cover (illustration, background); Bellwether Media, all interior backgrounds, pp. 4, 8, 11, 14-15, 15 (left, right), 16, 17 (left, right); Alpha/ Zuma Press, pp. 4-5; Carl Van Vechten/ Library of Congress, p. 7; Leonard McCombe/ Getty Images, pp. 8-9; Howard Liberman/ Library of Congress, p. 10; razorpix/ Alamy, p. 12 (left); AF Archive/ Alamy, p. 12 (right); ITV/ RexUSA, pp. 12-13; Evgeny Karandaev, pp. 14-15 (background); Glenn Copus/ Associated Newspapers/ RexUSA, pp. 18-19; FashionStock, p. 19.